THE GIVE AWAY CHILD

The Give Away Child

by

ANGELENA R WALLACE

Charleston, SC
www.PalmettoPublishing.com

The Give Away Child

Paperback ISBN: 978-1-68515-569-8
eBook ISBN: 978-1-68515-570-4

To anyone who is suffering from anger because of not having their parents while growing up.

Table of Contents

Introduction

Growing up as a child, my life was very challenging. I did not have any siblings to help me, so I had to do everything on my own. As an only child at home, I always wanted to tell stories. I love performing; just being able to be the one to make people laugh would make me happy. I was a firm believer that one day I would be able to tell this story to people all over the world.

CHAPTER ONE

The Journey Begins

It was a sad day in May 1970. A seven-and-a-half-month-old child was being given away to her aunt by her birth mother, who never returned to check on her.

The aunt, who did not own a home and lived on her father's property with a sick husband, did not know how to read or write. She had no job, but she helped other neighbors so she could get food for herself and the little girl. She did the best she could for the little girl with no help from the mother or father. At the age of three years old, the little girl started to go with her aunt to help the neighbors too so she herself could get something extra to eat, and the aunt could get a little more for food. She would pick oranges, peel ginger, pick mangoes, and do whatever was offered for them to do. When she reached the age of five years old, she started cleaning the neighbors' houses, so they got sufficient money for food. At the age of six years old, she was then registered into a primary school under a name that was not her birth certificate name. There was not any parent, and the aunt did not know her birth register name because she couldn't read.

She started cleaning more neighbors' houses so she could buy books for school. Since they could not afford to buy shoes, she had to cut out cardboard boxes and put strings into them to make a flip-flop so the road would not burn her feet. She was a very smart little girl and very bright in school, always getting first place in class. She started to stay back after school to help clean up the classrooms so the teachers would help her out with the buying of her books. Then when she reached home, she would clean the neighbors' houses so she could get dinner and lunch for school the next day.

At the age of twelve, she started asking questions about her parents because her aunt's husband told her that they were her uncle and aunt. He also told her to meet her grandmother, the mother of her birth mother. Her grandmother told her where her mother was living and that she was married with other children, so she started to see her grandmother every weekend. She got so active she started to communicate in sports at her school. She became a first place runner and then started running for the school. She was thirteen years old when her grandmother passed away.

CHAPTER TWO

Resisting the Pain

After the passing of her grandmother, she was so sad because she knew no other family member, just her aunt and uncle. She continued running for the school sport so she could get help with her school supplies. Her teacher became her fan, but she had been called the teacher's pet. Soon after, her uncle passed away, which weakened her spirit. She only had her aunt left, no mother, father, sister, or brother. She dropped out of school in tenth grade because her aunt became sickly. Her aunt gave her away to another family in the next town. She knew nobody there.

She started taking care of the new family's children and cleaning and working in their shop. They treated her as if she was nobody. She had to use the outside bathroom, was not allowed to sit at the dining table, and was introduced as the giveaway child. She felt sorry for herself and wanted to find her birth mother, so she remembered what her grandmother told her. She then went out begging the neighbors for money. She told them she wanted to find her birth mother. At the age of fifteen years old, when she got sufficient money, she went to find her mother, hoping she would be excited and glad to see her and welcome her home so she could start feeling what love is. So there she started her journey for almost twenty-four hours on a bus.

The bus driver then dropped her off and asked someone who knew her mother to take her to the address where she lived. She was so excited and anxiously waited for love. She turned up at her mother's home smiling, waiting to see what her mother looked like. She knocked, and a lady opened the door. She smiled and said, "I am your daughter," waiting for a hug and a welcome from her birth mother, but instead she was splashed with water in her face. Her birth mother then asked, "What are you doing here?" She pretended like nothing happened and made herself to believe that someone had provoked her mother, so she smiled again and said, "I am your daughter, Mom." The mother then slammed the door in her face and told her to go away.

She was so shocked she could not move with tears running down her eyes. She still was believing that her mother would come out and get her, at least talk to her, but instead it was a male who came to the door. He said hello, told her his name, and told her that he was the husband of her mother. He asked who she was, and she told him she was his wife's first child. He was surprised because her mother never mentioned to him that she had another child, so he went back inside. The giveaway child could hear him asking her about all the lies. Her mother came to the door and told her to get lost and to stay away from her and her family.

CHAPTER THREE

There Is Always Someone Who Cares

The stranger whom the bus driver asked to take her to her mother's house offered her to stay overnight because the bus would not come back until the next day. She gave the child a place to sleep and food to eat, allowed her to take a shower, and gave her bus fare to go back to where she came from. She started to worry because she took off from the other family without telling them where she was going and she didn't know if they would take her back if she told them she went to find her birth mother, so she started to tell the stranger all the information that was told to her about her father by her grandmother.

The stranger started asking questions until she heard something that led her to the police station because the giveaway child's father was a police officer by profession, so they went to the police station where her father worked. The stranger explained to the officer on duty the situation. There were five officers with the same name at the location, and he contacted all of them, and it was a blessing because the police officer who came to the station a few hours later was the giveaway child's father, and he hugged and welcomed her into his arms. The child had never received attention like that before and was happy.

The father then took the child, thanked the stranger, and took the child to his home, where she met a stepmother, a brother, and a baby sister. He told the stepmother how long he had been asking the birth mother about the giveaway child, but she refused to say anything, so all he did was give her child support and accept her wishes that she didn't want him in the child's life and did not have any idea that the child was given away. There was something that blew the child's mind. When all her siblings from her father heard about her, they started to treat her as if they had known her for a long time and as if they grew up together, which made the child very happy.

CHAPTER FOUR

Let's Fight a Good Fight

The giveaway child started meeting other family members from her father's side. She then found out that her registered name was different from the name that she had gone to school with because her father showed her a copy of her birth certificate. Her aunt could not be blamed for it because she had no contact with her birth mother and she herself could not read; she just wanted the best for the child. The child continued to use the name that she grew up to know for a while because sometimes when she had to sign paperwork, she tended to use the name she was used to, so it took her a while to get used to the name on the birth certificate and to even pronounce it.

Many times, when she was by herself, she would wonder why her birth mother did not want her, so when she grew up, nothing was simple for her. Life got hard for her as a young lady. When her father went to live with his wife in another state, she tried everything to make life comfortable for her. She communicated with her father, who always encouraged her to be strong. He would send her money whenever he could. She was very happy being able to communicate with her father. No birthday went by without her getting a call from him to tell her how special she was, and that was what gave her the strength to fight life. She always fell to the lowest point but kept finding a way to get back on her feet. She fought life with all the strength that she had.

CHAPTER FIVE

Things Already Better

The young lady found a way to make it to her father and stepmother. She did not like where her father was living, so her big brother came to get her and took her to his house. That was the worst mistake she had ever done. Life made a turn for the worse because her brother ended up putting her out of the apartment, and she had to live on the street for a while, sleeping under the bus shed in the winter. She ended up in a government shelter facility, and that was when she started having seizures. She took a more effective tool on her because she could not walk for an hour without falling in the street and ending up in the emergency.

It took a very hard toll on the young lady. She started to think very hard about what she was going through. The doctors could not find the seizure; they just knew that the symptoms was that of a seizure, so the doctors had to pull her out of work. Things got worse, and because she had no finances, she became homeless. She took it so hard that she started thinking about suicide. One day she decided that she would walk out into a driving bus. She kept hearing a voice telling her to walk out into it when the bus was close. As she attempted to do so, she heard another voice call her by name. She turned around to see who it was, but as the bus passed by, no one was there, so she knew that got to be a call from God himself.

She was invited to a church by a close friend. She did not want to go at first because she thought that God had forgotten about her, but he kept asking her every time he saw her until one day she told him she would visit for just one time so he could leave her alone. That was the best decision she had ever made.

CHAPTER SIX

The Best Is Yet to Come

She went with him that day thinking that was the only time that she would do it for him, but the Lord worked that day, and the young lady felt the presence of the Lord. She got saved that day and received the gift of the Holy Ghost. She decided to get baptized in the name of Jesus Christ, and from that day everything was changed in the young lady's life. Her seizure was gone, she brought her own house and a new vehicle, and God has been working in the young lady's life, blessing on top of blessing.

She had a church family who was very caring and always there for her, so she started to get her faith back. She had hope again. The mountain was still there to climb, but she had more strength to hold on. The pastor and his wife at the church treated her like she was their child, and that encouraged her to stay in Christ Jesus. She was so thankful and continued to praise God and minister what he had done for her. The more she praises him, the more the blessings increase. She felt herself and what Jesus had ordained her to do. She ministered every way she knew how, meeting people and telling them of where the Lord brought her from and showing others through videos on social media. She said, "If the Lord can do it for me, then he can do it for anyone. Don't give up. Never underestimate the power of God. There is power in the blood of Jesus."

She could leave her house now and not worry about ending up in the emergency from a fall in the street from seizure because God had taken it all away. She could start driving again with no worry because God was by her side. The friend who invited her to church was really a godsent. Even though she was always angry because of growing up as a giveaway child, always ready to fight as soon as someone said anything to hurt her feeling, he never stopped until she started to change her attitude and come to church with him. The road was not going to be easy for the young lady sometimes, but she now had the strength to hold on and prayed in Jesus's name.

CHAPTER SEVEN

Don't Give Up

After things were bright and everything was going good, she was now being contacted by her birth mother. At first she did not want to have anything to do with her, but Jesus Christ was living inside her, so she prayed and asked God to give her the strength to forgive her. She started speaking with her birth mother on the phone. She would call the young lady every day, and so the young lady fasted and prayed. She was able to speak with her without feeling any hate. They started to speak on a regular basis, and her birth mother would tell her what was going on in her life. She even ended up paying bills for her birth mother without thinking twice about it, and so God began to bless her more as she cared.

It happened when one day she decided to ask her about what happened so she could have a closure on her part. She asked her birth mother what caused her to give her away. She told her that her father was not helping her, so the young lady asked her why she never came back to check on her all those years. She started to cry, and so she told her birth mother to put it behind them and move forward, and that was what they did so they could have a relationship.

If you have faith and wait upon the Lord, he will see you through. "They that wait upon the Lord shall renew their strength; they shall mount up with wings as eagles; they shall run, and not be weary; and they shall walk, and not faint" (Isa. 40:31, KJV). Just teach me Lord how to wait. There are going to be difficult times, but if you only believe, you will make it to the end of the way. Don't give up, hold on to the end, and if you come to the end of the rope, don't jump off. Make a knot and hold on, think about your dreams and who you are meant to be, pray and ask God for help, and the journey will get smoother with less traffic. Hold on strong. Don't give up now. He is the same God, and he will never fail us. Have faith in him. You will make it in the end.

Acknowledgment

I want to thank my son, Polando Francis, for being my main support in this journey. He never gave up on me, pushing me forward, telling me he wanted to hear about the giveaway child so he could read it to his children. He would stay up with me at night on the phone and watch me write and remind me I was not the only person who needed to know the story. He expressed his love for me so I would not give up.

To my daughter, Nastacia Forrest, whose continued encouragement also tasked me to completing this story, always telling me how many people are going to be helped, those who are weak and need a word from this book.

To my pastor and his wife, who never gave up on me when I was sad, always finding a way to cheer me up.

Thank you, all. Your continued love and support is what brought me through to this moment. I couldn't have done it without you.

www.ingramcontent.com/pod-product-compliance
Ingram Content Group UK Ltd.
Pitfield, Milton Keynes, MK11 3LW, UK
UKHW020416250726
13967UKWH00007B/2663

9 781685 155698